Published by

James H. Kaster

Concord, NC

Printed in the United States of America

ISBN: 978-0-982-82206-7

The information contained within this book is true and complete to the best of my knowledge. Material was gathered from manufacturers' brochures, advertisements and media kits. Information is provided without any guarantee on the part of the publisher. Publisher also disclaims any liability incurred from use of this information.

© 2010 by James H. Kaster

All rights reserved. No part of this publication may be reproduced or transmitted in any form or by any means, electronic or mechanical, including photocopy, scanning, recording or any information retrieval system without permission in writing from the publisher. Permission is never granted for commercial purposes.

Manufacturer, vehicle, model, trim names and/or designations are the trademarks of the respective companies. They are used for identification purposes only. This is not an official publication of any of these companies or manufacturers.

Table of Contents

Table of Contents	2
Foreword	3
The 80's Measured	4
1980	5
1981	15
1982	27
1983	36
1984	47
1985	55
1986	64
1987	72
1988	81
1989	89
Index	97

Chapters are organized by year and then alphabetically by manufacturer within year. See the Index for a list of manufacturers within each year.

1980 Plymouth Horizon TC3 with Sports Appearance Package & Horizon 4-door

Foreword

The 80's. Like many of the decades before it, it was a decade of change. As the disco era was coming to a close, the glamour cars representing that time were becoming obsolete. Over the 80's decade, the industry began phasing out vinyl roofs, opera windows, opera lights, velour upholstery and other remnants of glitz. (Although pillow-type seats remained very popular in upper level trim cars.) Consumers demanded more function and feedback from their cars. As a result, cars became more driver-oriented, without sacrificing comfort.

The 80's. Unlike, the times before, however, it was a time when lines blurred even more. Re-badged, foreign assembled vehicles were sold on domestic car lots. Were cars considered "domestic" based on their assembly point or their content of U.S. made components? Did it matter as long as the profits went to a U.S. globally headquartered corporation? This debate still continues today.

Much like the blurring line of domestic/foreign definitions was the blurring of vehicle lines. In this decade we saw the introduction of the minivan with the Dodge Caravan/Plymouth Voyager and the introduction of the SUV by Jeep Cherokee. Though the manufacturers classified these vehicles as light trucks, they were used mostly by families with needs to haul people and their "stuff", replacing the role of the station wagon.

Trends in society found their ways into automobiles. Video game consoles became more popular and personal computers began appearing on household desks. A great use of electronics permeated in cars from controlling various mechanical systems to displaying instrumentation in digital readouts and even warning systems that talked.

The economy and a second gas crisis also had a significant impact, shaping manufacturers' responses throughout the 80's. Cars shrank in size and engine displacements. Many platforms migrated to front-wheel drive. And with a few years of experience building smaller cars, auto companies learned how to make smaller engines more powerful through an increased use of turbo-charging.

Yet, in the 80's, there were some contrasts. While cars continued to downsize and follow function, hairstyles grew. Women wore large, frizzy, crimped and messy styles while men wore mullets (business in the front, party in the back).

I began the 80's in college, studying computer science. Secretly, I pondered whether I should have considered more seriously a career in the automotive industry. There was just something about automobiles that kept my focus. Yet, my interest in computer technology proved equally strong. While software applications became a career, automobiles would become my passion.

The 80's, like 2008-2010 (the time of this composition) was a time of economic strife that threatens the survival of the U.S. auto industry. We find that Chrysler's survival, yet again, depends on government intervention. Yet, the struggle for the industry goes beyond Chrysler. GM is on life support, also using taxpayer money to rebuild. Chrysler survived the 80's and came out a stronger, more profitable corporation. It is yet to be seen if the same scenario holds true for Chrysler and GM as the economy of the Great Recession recovers.

As a young boy, my father inspired my passion for automobiles. We spent Sundays (there were blue laws then) on car lots, free from salespeople. We looked at cars, considered their styles, materials, features and options. We compared and noted other manufacturer's comparable vehicles to each car we studied. There was something we could find to appreciate in a base Pinto as well as the top of the line Lincoln. It wasn't about horsepower. For us, it was about the artistry of design, the folds and creases in the metal, styling cues that paid loyal homage to previous generations, extra comforts and conveniences, appointments and new technologies.

Today, my modest collection of cars include four cars from the 80's: the last year of the Lincoln Versailles, a Mercury Cougar XR-7, a Chrysler LeBaron Mark Cross convertible and a Chrysler LeBaron Mark Cross turbo coupe. I delight in driving them as they are now unique on the roads and reliable for everyday driving.

I hope you enjoy this trip through the 80's memory lane as much as I enjoy compiling the material.

James H. Kaster

The 80's Measured

The chart below shows the pattern of costs for various items throughout the decade. While the cost of bread was increasing, the cost of gasoline was decreasing and by the middle of the decade, a loaf of bread cost more than a gallon of gasoline. Housing prices made a big jump in 1989. Together, these two metrics ushered in the 90's SUV craze. Homeowners, using their newfound equity, took out second mortgages to purchase larger cars and SUVs than had been available in the 80's. With gas prices so low, the MPG concerns that started the early 80's recession was no longer a concern by the end of the decade. Interestingly, as we enter the 2010 & 2011 model years, we find ourselves in a similar, if not worse, predicament. The U.S. is in its most severe recession since World War II and the volatile cost of gasoline has consumers demanding fuel efficient vehicles. History is repeating.

Cost Comparison Chart

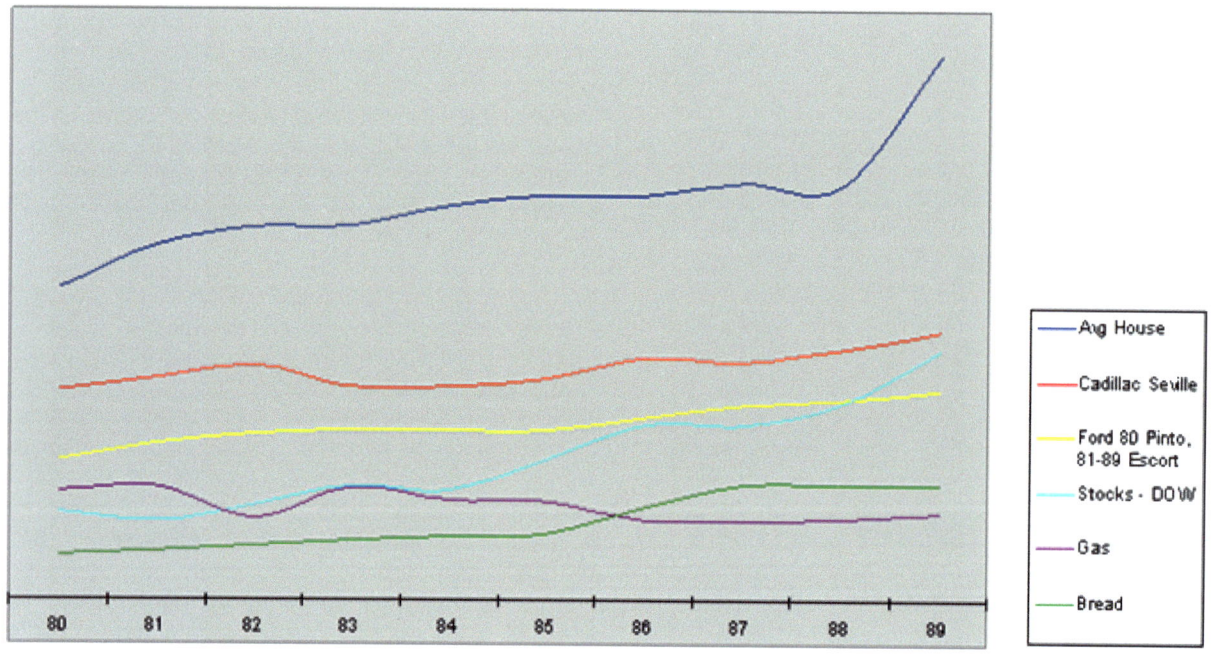

Percentage of change, comparing 1989 to 1980

Average House Price	74.7%
Cadillac Seville	29.1%
Ford '89 Escort / '80 Pinto	51.2%
Stocks – DOW	185.0%
Gallon of Gas	-18.5%
Loaf of Bread	168.6%

1980

1980 - Facts at Glance

News Headlines

- US operation failed to free hostages in Iran
- Ronald Reagan elected President
- Mount St. Helen Erupts
- John Lennon is killed
- Fire destroys MGM Grand Hotel in Las Vegas
- Winter Olympics held in Lake Placid
- Pac-Man introduced

Tops in Pop Culture

Music
- Call Me, Blondie

Movies
- Star Wars Episode V: The Empire Strikes Back

TV Show
- Dallas

Sports Champions

Basketball
- LA Lakers

Football
- Pittsburg Steelers

Baseball
- Philadelphia Phillies

MT – Car of the Year

Chevrolet Citation

Those 80s Cars – AMC & Chrysler

1980 - AMC / EAGLE

1980 AMC Concord Limited Wagon

1980 AMC Concord Limited Sedan

1980 AMC Concord DL Coupe

1980 AMC Concord available leather interior

1980 AMC Concord instrument panel

1980 AMC Spirit Limited leather interior

Standard G.T. Rally-tuned suspension system

Last Model Run: 1980 AMC AMX

1980 AMC Spirit Sedan

2.5 liter 4-cylinder power

1980 AMC Eagle Sedan

1980 AMC Spirit Liftback

1980 AMC Eagle Sport Wagon, 2-door & 4-door

Last Model Run: 1980 AMC Pacer Sedan

Last Model Run: 1980 AMC Pacer Wagon

Those 80s Cars – AMC & Chrysler

1980 - CHRYSLER

5.2 liter V8 (318) standard & 5.9 liter (360) optional

1980 Chrysler New Yorker Fifth Avenue

From the Brochure: "Every facet of its brilliant design speaks eloquently for itself. The long, graceful sweep of its classic profile. The understated beauty of its chrome grille topped by the striking pentastar hood ornament. Concealed headlamps."
– 1980 Chrysler New Yorker

1980 Chrysler New Yorker instrument panel

1980 Chrysler New Yorker Standard Richton cloth interior

1980 Chrysler Newport interior

3.7 liter (225) slant six standard on Newport; 5.2 liter V8 (318) & 5.9 liter (360) optional

1980 Chrysler Newport

From the Brochure: "Friend. Seldom has the term been more appropriate in describing a car. The right car at the right time. A Chrysler in the true sense. Capably equipped, superbly appointed and yet so wonderfully affordable in light of its standard attributes."
– 1980 Chrysler Newport

3.7 liter (225) slant six standard & 5.2 liter V8 (318) optional

112.7" wheelbase
209.8" length
3,362 lbs

New Model: 1980 Chrysler Cordoba

1980 Chrysler Cordoba crest

New trim: Crown Corinthian Edition with exclusive Black Walnut Metallic or Designer's Cream-on-Beige paint treatments.

1980 Chrysler Cordoba instrument panel with tilt steering wheel

1980 Chrysler Cordoba available leather interior

From the Brochure: "Cordoba 1980. A car whose striking new resized form strides into the new decade with poise and assurance befitting its proud tradition. From its Franklin Minted hood ornament to its tri-lens taillamps, Cordoba 1980 is an exceptional automobile. But extraordinary styling marks the beginning.

Cordoba. The car that redefined the term "contemporary classic" during the 1970's returns to set new standards of personal luxury for the 1980's."

– 1980 Chrysler Cordoba

Those 80s Cars – AMC & Chrysler

3.7 liter (225) slant six standard & 5.2 liter V8 (318) optional

2-doors shortened to a 108.7" wheelbase

Refreshed: 1980 Chrysler LeBaron LS

1980 Chrysler LeBaron LS instrument panel

1980 Chrysler LeBaron 4-door

From the Brochure: "The whole idea of elegance in a personal-sized car is rapidly changing Chrysler LeBaron has a great deal to do with this changing attitude."
– 1980 Chrysler LeBaron

1980 Chrysler LeBaron bucket seat interior option

1980 Chrysler LeBaron Town & Country

1980 - DODGE

1980 Dodge Diplomat S-Type bucket seat interior, 4-door sedan, illuminated entry, electronic stereo

Diplomat & Mirada: 3.7 liter (225) slant six standard & 5.2 liter V8 (318) optional

Refreshed: 1980 Dodge Diplomat S-Type 2-door Coupe

1980 Dodge Diplomat Salon Wagon

6 different Aspen coupe series

Last Model Run: 1980 Dodge Aspen Value Sedan & Sunrise Coupe

New Model: 1980 Dodge Mirada

Aspen pricing starts under $5,000

Last Model Run: 1980 Dodge Aspen Special Edition Wagon

1980 Dodge St. Regis

New for 1980: Touring Edition series
Touring Edition instrument cluster shown

1980 Dodge St. Regis interior, instrument panel & optional glass sunroof

1980 Dodge Omni 024

1.7 liter 4-cylinder w/4-speed manual are standard

1.6 liter & 2.6 liter 4-cylinder engines

1980 Dodge Challenger

1980 Dodge Omni 4-door with Premium Exterior Package

1980 Dodge Colt Custom Hatchback with RS Package & Colt Station Wagon

2.6 liter 4-cylinder standard on wagon

12 Those 80s Cars – AMC & Chrysler

1980 - PLYMOUTH

Optional 5.9 liter 4bbl V8

New Model: 1980 Plymouth Gran Fury Pursuit Package

3.7 liter Slant Six, 5.2 liter V8 & 5.9 liter V8 engine options

New Model: 1980 Plymouth Gran Fury

Last Model Run: 1980 Plymouth Volare 4-door with Premier Package

2-doors: Volare, Custom, Special, Premier, & Duster
4-doors: Volare, Custom, Special, Premier
Wagons: Volare, Custom & Premier

1980 Plymouth Gran Fury interior and optional features

3.7 liter Slant Six & 5.2 liter V8

Last Model Run: 1980 Plymouth Duster

1980 Plymouth Volare with all-vinyl 60/40 seats

1980 Plymouth Volare instrument panel

Last Model Run: 1980 Plymouth Volare Wagon with Custom Package

Those 80s Cars – AMC & Chrysler   13

Last Model Run: Plymouth Arrow (1979 above)

Last Model Run: 1980 Plymouth Arrow

1980 Plymouth Horizon TC3 with Sports Appearance Package & Horizon 4-door

1.7 liter 4-cylinder w/4-speed manual are standard

1980 Plymouth Horizon Custom Interior Package (woodgrain dash appliqués, locking glove box, cigarette lighter, knit-cloth covered headliner, custom door trim, rear armrests, custom vinyl bucket seats)

1980 Plymouth Horizon instrument panel with optional deep-dish 4-spoke sport steering wheel

2.6 liter 4-cylinder

1980 Plymouth Sapporo

1980 Plymouth Horizon with Premium Woodgrain Package

1981

1981 - Facts at Glance

News Headlines

- Reagan fires striking air traffic controllers
- Researchers find the wreck of the Titanic
- Muhammad Ali retires
- Lady Diana marries Prince Charles
- Egyptian President Anwar Sadat is assassinated
- Sandra Day O'Connor appointed to Supreme Court
- 1st test tube baby is born
- Microsoft introduces MS-DOS
- MTV launched

Tops in Pop Culture

Music
- Bette Davis Eyes, Kim Carnes

Movies
- Raiders of the Lost Ark

TV Show
- Dallas

Sports Champions

Basketball
- Boston Celtics

Football
- Oakland Raiders

Baseball
- L.A. Dodgers

Motor Trend – Car of the Year

Chrysler K Cars:
Dodge Aries & Plymouth Reliant

Those 80s Cars – AMC & Chrysler

1981 - AMC / EAGLE

1981 AMC Spirit Hatchback & 2-door Sedan

1981 AMC Spirit interior

1981 AMC Spirit instrument panel

1981 AMC Spirit interior

1981 AMC Concord Station Wagon

1981 AMC Concord 4-door Sedan

1981 AMC Concord DL interior

1981 AMC wheels and wheel covers

From the Brochure: "Choose a Spirit for its substance or its style and get a full measure of both. Spirit interiors, in particular, are better equipped and appointed than those in many other small cars." — 1981 AMC Spirit

1981 AMC Eagle 4-door

1981 AMC Eagle 2-door

Press Kit: "The 1981 Eagle 2-dr. and 4-dr. sedan offer a combination of luxury and the convenience of a compact with the superior traction and handling of four-wheel drive. For 1981, American Motors leads the U.S. auto industry with another first and exclusive. All Eagle models utilize 100 percent one-side galvanized steel on all exterior body panels. A 2.5 liter 4-cylinder engine is standard, with 4.2 liter 6-cylinder engine optional."

– 1981 AMC Eagle

1981 AMC Eagle SX/4

1981 AMC Eagle Kammback

1981 AMC Eagle Station Wagon

1981 AMC Eagle 4-door & 2-door Sedans

1981 AMC AMX Turbo Pace Car

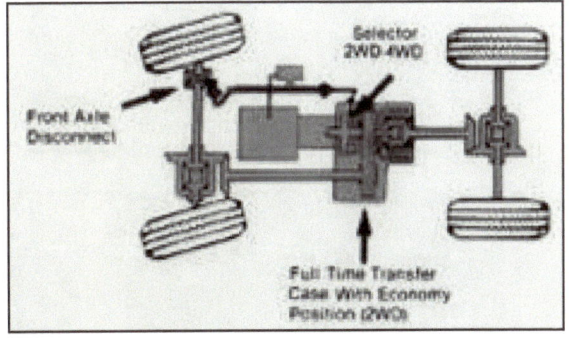

Press Kit: "The AMX Turbo Pace Car is an exclusive – the personal design of Richard A. Teague, American Motor's Vice President of Automotive Design. This two-passenger, aerodynamically efficient vehicle will be one of four official pace cars in the PPG Indy Car World Series during the 1981 racing season."

– 1981 AMX Turbo

Those 80s Cars – AMC & Chrysler

1981 - CHRYSLER / IMPERIAL

5.2 liter V8 with EFI

It's time for Imperial.

New Model: 1981 Imperial

9-button trip computer

1981 Imperial instrument panel

1981 Imperial Mark Cross leather interior

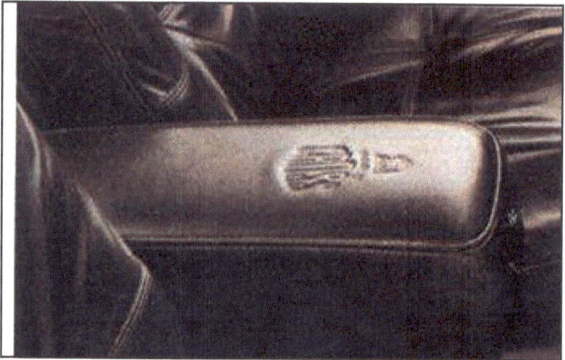

1981 Imperial Mark Cross leather interior

1981 Imperial Cartier Crystal Pentastar

From the Brochure: "No other American automobile offers as complete a list of standard luxury features as Imperial. Including WSW steel-belted radial tires; Goodyear all-weather Arriva or Michelin. A choice of four sophisticated sounds systems. Speed Control. All power assists. Individually adjustable power seats. Sophisticated electronic instrumentation. There is only one extra-cost option: an electrically powered sliding roof. The 1981 Imperial is America's totally equipped personal luxury car."

- 1981 Imperial

Last Model Run: 1981 Chrysler New Yorker

Last Model Run: 1981 Chrysler Newport

1981 Chrysler Newport interior

1981 Chrysler Cordoba Corinthian Package

1981 Chrysler Cordoba instrument panel

1981 Chrysler New Yorker interior

1981 Chrysler New Yorker instrument panel

1981 Chrysler Cordoba standard interior

1981 Chrysler Cordoba with optional Cabriolet Roof and two-tone paint treatment

1981 Chrysler Cordoba LS

Those 80s Cars – AMC & Chrysler

Last Model Run: 1981 Chrysler LeBaron Medallion 4-door Sedan

1981 Chrysler LeBaron interior

Last Model Run: 1981 Chrysler LeBaron Town & Country Wagon

Last Model Run: 1981 Chrysler LeBaron 2-door

1981 Chrysler LeBaron instrument panel

From the Brochure: "LeBaron for 1981 carries with it an unmistakable air of space-efficient elegance. And LeBaron pairs the promise of its looks with the performance of its Super Six 2-barrel engine, the driving ease and convenience of Torqueflite automatic transmission, power steering, power front disc brakes and a host of other standard features.

Pick your car from LeBaron – a new price class – or LeBaron Medallion. Both categories provide two-door specialty hardtops and four-door sedans. If you have a penchant for station wagons, the LeBaron Town & Country is outstanding."

- 1981 Chrysler LeBaron

1981 - DODGE

Last Model Run: 1981 Dodge St. Regis

1981 Dodge St. Regis instrument panel

1981 Dodge St. Regis standard cloth interior

From the Brochure: "It's a beautiful way to close off the outside world. Just being inside St. Regis is something special – the quiet, the comfort, and the luxury. Quality surrounds you in excellence of design, tasteful selection of materials, careful attention to detail. But most importantly, St. Regis signifies outstanding value, because the 1981 St. Regis offers a higher appointment level and more standard equipment than last year's model."

- 1981 Dodge St. Regis

1981 Dodge Mirada with CMX Package

Chrysler Corporation offers a 30 day, 1,000 mile money-back guarantee

1981 Dodge Mirada

1981 Dodge Mirada with optional leather interior

2.2 liter OHC 4-cylinder

New Model: 1981 Dodge Aries SE 4-door

1981 Dodge Aries SE instrument panel

New Model: 1981 Dodge Aries SE 4-door Wagon

New Model: 1981 Dodge Aries optional Premium cloth bucket seats and console

Those 80s Cars – AMC & Chrysler

Last Model Run: 1981 Dodge Diplomat Sport Coupe

73.3 cu. ft. of cargo space

Last Model Run: 1981 Dodge Diplomat Salon Wagon

1981 Dodge Diplomat Salon 2-door optional cloth and vinyl bucket seat interior

1981 Dodge Diplomat Medallion 4-door Sedan

1981 Dodge Colt RS

1981 Dodge Challenger

From the Brochure: "Colt RS: efficiency and a whole lot more. The Colt RS takes the Colt Custom and adds even more sportiness – from the Red and Black two-tone paint to the Yellow and Orange accent stripes. Now, attack any road with a 1.6-liter MCA-JET four-cylinder engine, sure-footed front-wheel-drive and the nimble Rallye Handling Package."

1981 Dodge Omni with Custom Exterior Package

From the Brochure: "Consider our 1981 Dodge Omni for a minute. Its transverse-engine, front-wheel-drive design gives Omni interior room to spare for five adult-size passengers… with four doors to get them in and out with a minimum of fuss, and a convenient rear hatch and folding rear seats to turn back-seat space into cargo space. Omni is built with computers and precise automated welders in one of the country's most modern assembly plants and is powered by one of two four cylinder engines… the standard 1.7 liter or the optional Chrysler-designed-and-built 2.2 liter Trans-4."
- 1981 Dodge Omni

1981 Dodge 024 with Sports Appearance Package

1981 Dodge Omni optional Premium interior

From the Brochure: "Let's take it from the 'top.' The 024's superbly streamlined, aerodynamically designed body actually helps curb wind resistance on the highway, improving gas mileage. From its sleek front end to its roomy cargo area, you'll get an extraordinary ride without overextending your fuel budget."
– 1981 Dodge 024

1981 Dodge Omni Rallye instrument cluster & four spoke steering wheel

1981 - PLYMOUTH

New Model: 1981 Plymouth Reliant SE 4-door

2.2 liter OHC 4-cylinder

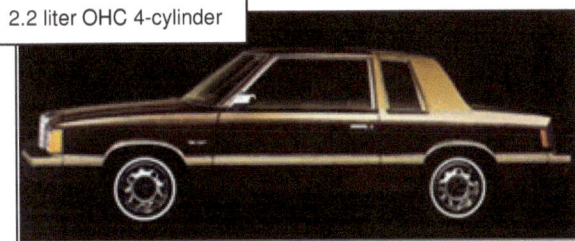
New Model: 1981 Plymouth Reliant SE 2-door

New Model: 1981 Plymouth Reliant SE Wagon

1981 Plymouth Reliant SE instrument panel

1981 Plymouth Sapporo

Sapporo interior: durable cord velour cloth-and-vinyl reclining bucket seats with integral, adjustable headrests and driver side lumbar adjust

Last Model Run: 1981 Plymouth Gran Fury

1981 Plymouth Gran Fury interior

1981 Plymouth Reliant SE standard bench seat

1981 Plymouth Sapporo interior

1.7 liter 4-cylinder w/4-speed manual

1981 Plymouth TC3 with Sport Two-Tone Package

1981 Plymouth TC3 with Custom Exterior Package

Euro-Sedan: black-out exterior trim, wide tires, cast-aluminum road wheels, Sport Interior, Rallye instruments

1981 Plymouth Horizon Euro-Sedan

1.4 liter 4-cylinder w/4-speed manual. EPA estimated 37 MPG, 50 hwy

1981 Plymouth Champ Custom with LS Package

1981 Plymouth Horizon with Custom Exterior

From the Brochure: "Engineered and built with care by Mitsubishi Motors Corporation in Japan, the 1981 front-wheel drive Plymouth Champ lineup offers three ways to go! Beginning with the basic, highest-mileage Champ, Champ Deluxe and Champ Custom, there's a Champ that's just right for you."
- 1981 Plymouth Champ

From the Brochure: "Meet the highest mileage, lowest priced Horizon for 1981. (Not available in California.) It offers the same front-wheel-drive technology, full five-passenger seating, folding rear seat and handy rear hatch design shared by all our 1981 Horizons. Plus a specially calibrated version of our standard 1.7-liter four-cylinder engine and a special 2.69 overall top gear ratio with standard four-speed manual transaxle."
- 1981 Plymouth Horizon

1982

1982 - Facts at Glance

News Headlines

- Falkland war ignites
- USA Today launched
- Disney's EPCOT center opens
- 1st artificial heart transplanted
- Vietnam Veterans Memorial dedicated

Tops in Pop Culture

Music
- Physical, Olivia Newton-John

Movies
- ET: The Extra-Terrestrial

TV Show
- 60 Minutes

Sports Champions

Basketball
- L.A. Lakers

Football
- San Francisco 49ers

Baseball
- St. Louis Cardinals

Motor Trend – Car of the Year

Chevrolet Camaro Z28

1982 - AMC / EAGLE

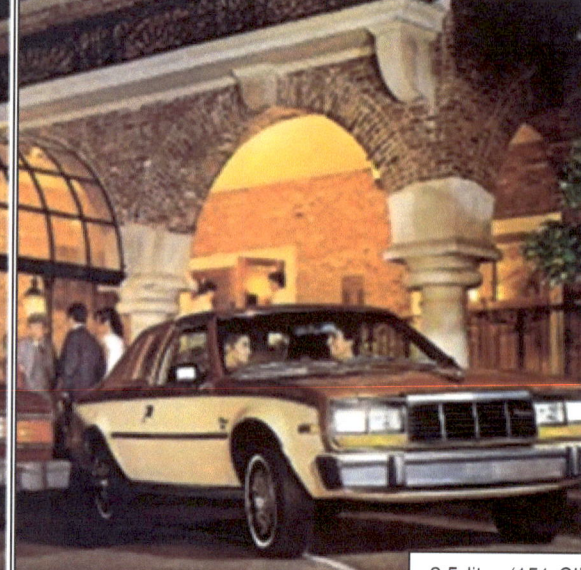

1982 AMC Concord DL 4-door Sedan and Concord Limited 2-door Sedan

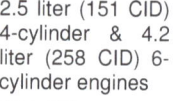

2.5 liter (151 CID) 4-cylinder & 4.2 liter (258 CID) 6-cylinder engines

1982 AMC Spirit G.T. Liftback

Manual 5-speed transmission with gauge package

1982 AMC Eagle SX/4, Wagon & 4-door Sedan

1982 Concord DL Wagons

Tilt steering wheel

AMC Concord & Eagle Limited interior (top)
AMC Spirit & Eagle SX/4 DL interior (bottom)

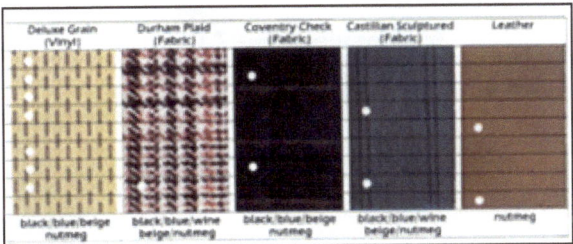

1982 AMC & Eagle upholstery options

1982 AMC Eagle 4-door Sedan & 2-door Coupe

1982 AMC & Eagle wheel & cover choices

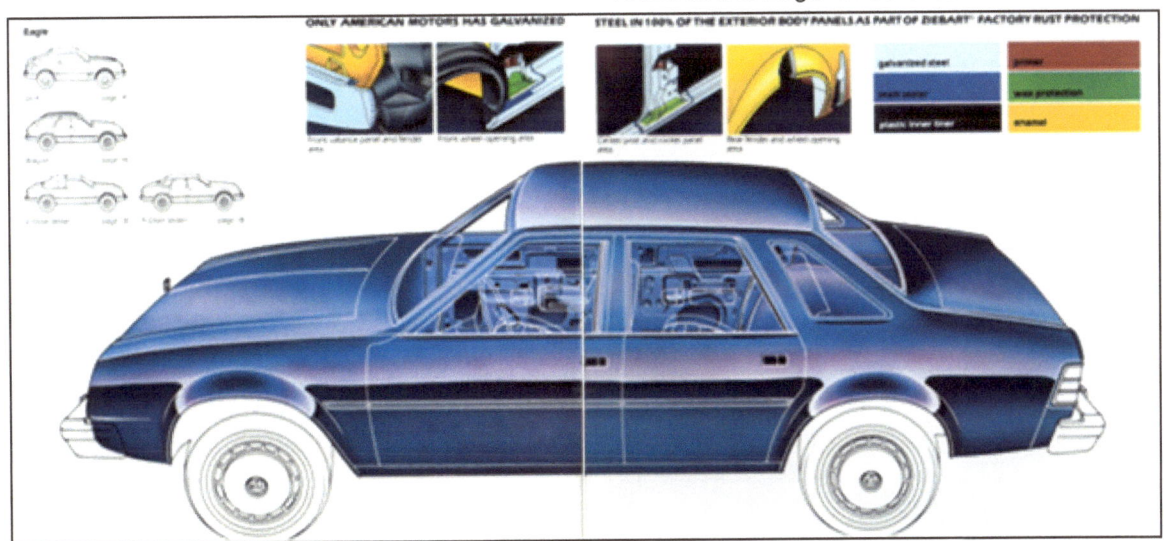

Those 80s Cars – AMC & Chrysler

1982 - CHRYSLER / IMPERIAL

New Model: 1982 Chrysler Town & Country

New Model: 1982 Chrysler LeBaron Medallion 2-door Coupe

LeBaron: now front-wheel drive with 2.2 liter (135 CID) standard and a Mitsubishi-built 2.6 liter (156 CID) optional

New Model: 1982 Chrysler LeBaron Mark Cross convertible

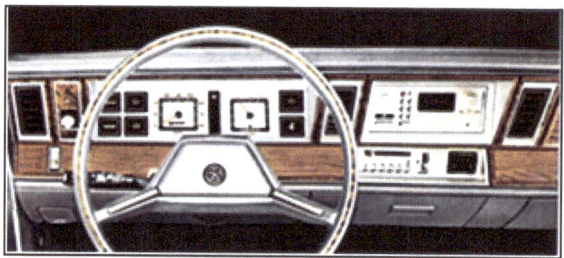
1982 Chrysler LeBaron instrument panel

1982 Chrysler LeBaron Medallion interior

99.9" wheelbase, 179.7" length weighing just under 2,500 lbs

New Model: 1982 Chrysler LeBaron Medallion 4-door Sedan

1982 Chrysler Cordoba

New Model: 1982 Chrysler New Yorker

1981's LeBaron is re-styled and re-branded as 1982's replacement for the New Yorker

1982 Chrysler Cordoba instrument panel

1982 Chrysler Cordoba cloth interior

1982 Chrysler New Yorker cloth interior

1982 Chrysler New Yorker instrument panel

1982 Imperial instrument panel

1982 Imperial cloth interior

New Series: 1982 Imperial FS (Frank Sinatra)

Those 80s Cars – AMC & Chrysler 31

1982 - DODGE

New Model: 1982 Dodge 400 LS 2-door Coupe

Front-wheel drive with 2.2 liter, optional Mitsubishi-built 2.6 liter

New Model: 1982 Dodge 400 LS 4-door Sedan

1982 Dodge Omni

26 EPA estimated MPG
41 MPG highway

1982 Dodge Aries SE 4-door Sedan, Aries Custom 2-door Sedan, Aries SE Wagon

New Model: 1982 Dodge 400 Convertible

Challenger 2.6 liter & 5-speed manual transmission standard

1982 Dodge imports: Challenger, Colt RS, Colt Custom 4-door Hatchback

1982 Dodge Charger 2.2

2.2 liter w/4-speed manual or 3-speed auto

New Model: 1982 Dodge Rampage

1982 Dodge Diplomat

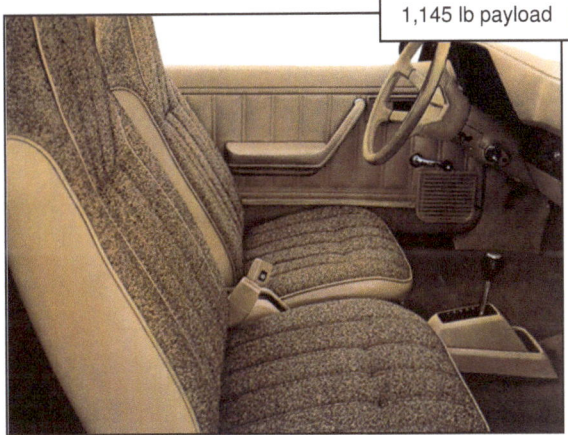

1,145 lb payload

1982 Dodge Rampage optional cloth interior

16.7 cu. ft. trunk, 18-gallon fuel tank

1982 Dodge Mirada with T-Bar Roof

Those 80s Cars – AMC & Chrysler

1982 - PLYMOUTH

3.7 liter 2-bbl Slant Six w/3-speed auto are standard

New Model: 1982 Plymouth Gran Fury (based on stable-mate design, Dodge Diplomat)

New Model: 1982 Plymouth Gran Fury

33.9 cu. ft. cargo space

1982 Plymouth Turismo

1982 Plymouth Gran Fury interior

2.6 liter 4-cylinder w/5-speed manual

1982 Plymouth Sapporo

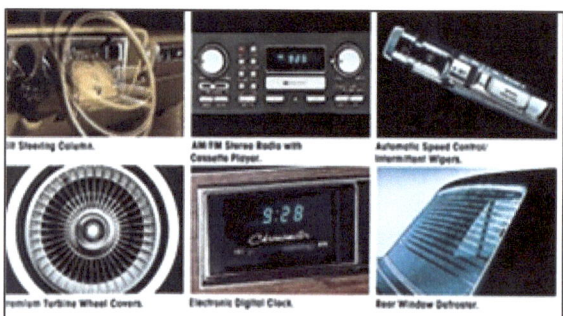

1982 Plymouth Gran Fury options

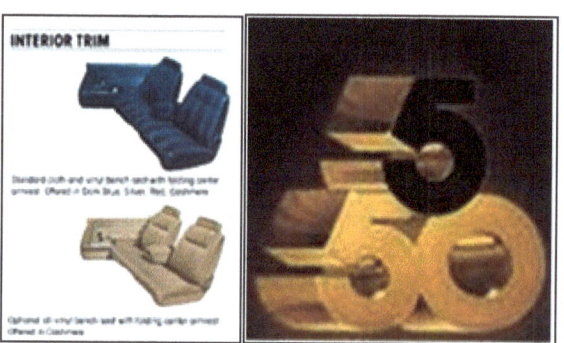

Fury seating & Chrysler Corporation's 5/50 Protection Plan

1982 Plymouth Reliant SE 2-door Coupe

1982 Plymouth Reliant SE interior

1982 Plymouth Reliant SE Wagon

1982 Plymouth Reliant Custom 4-door Sedan

1982 Plymouth Horizon Custom

1982 Plymouth Champ Custom with LS Package

From the Brochure: "What are Americans demanding in a car today? Fuel economy, high-quality design and construction and reliability... in a word: value. We think they'll find it all in one American car: the well-built 1982 Plymouth Reliant that's rated at 26 EPA est MPG, 41 estimated highway."

- 1982 Plymouth Reliant

1983

1983 - Facts at Glance

News Headlines

- Motorola introduces mobile phones in the United States
- Sally Ride becomes 1st American woamn in space
- IBM introduces PC XT
- MS Word & Lotus 1-2-3 are released
- Cabbage Patch Doll is introduced

Tops in Pop Culture

Music
- Every Breath You Take, The Police

Movies
- Star Wars Episode VI: Return of the Jedi

TV Show
- Dallas

Sports Champions

Basketball
- Philadelphia 76ers

Football
- Washington Redskins

Baseball
- Baltimore Orioles

Motor Trend – Car of the Year

AMC/Renault Alliance

1983 - AMC / EAGLE

1983 AMC Spirit DL Liftback & Concord Limited Wagon

1983 AMC Concord DL Sedan and Concord DL Wagon

1983 AMC Spirit GT Liftback

1983 AMC Spirit GT Liftback

1983 AMC / Eagle & Renault

1983 Eagle SX/4

1983 Eagle Sedan & Wagon

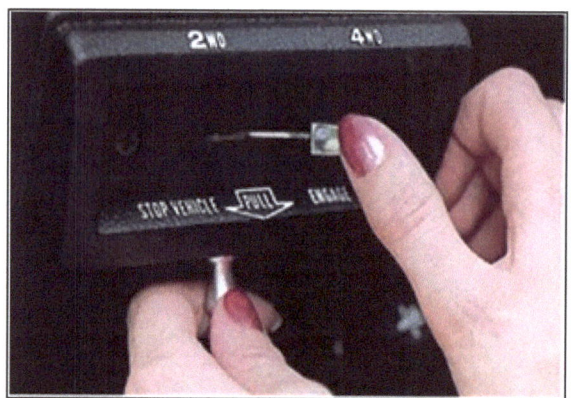
1983 Eagle

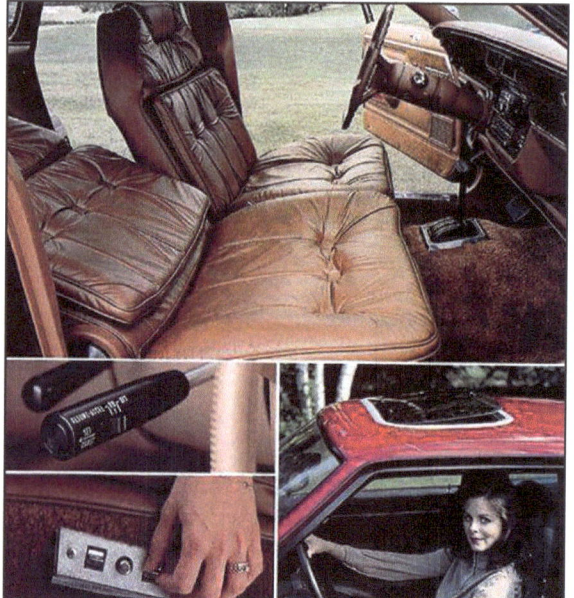
1983 AMC / Eagle options

1983 Renault Alliance sold at AMC Dealers (Renault purchased AMC / Eagle / Jeep)

1983 Renault Fuego sold at AMC dealers

1983 - CHRYSLER / IMPERIAL

1983 Imperial optional leather interior

Last Model Run: 1983 Imperial

1983 Imperial instrument panel

1983 Imperial features

Last Model Run: 1983 Imperial

1983 Chrysler New Yorker Fifth Avenue

1982's New Yorker is re-branded as 1983 New Yorker Fifth Avenue to make room for a new front-drive New Yorker

1983 Chrysler New Yorker Fifth Avenue optional leather interior

1983 Chrysler New Yorker Fifth Avenue instrument panel

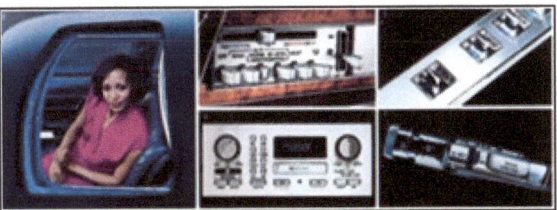
1983 Chrysler New Yorker Fifth Avenue features

Those 80s Cars – AMC & Chrysler

1983 Chrysler E Class instrument panel & optional interior (standard on New Yorker)

2.2 liter (135 CID) standard and a Mitsubishi-built 2.6 liter (156 CID) is optional on both E Class & New Yorker

From the Brochure: "Chrysler's largest front-wheel drive sedan. Chrysler E Class, America's newest front-wheel drive automobile, offers a highly desirable combination of six-passenger room, outstanding ride and handling, and superb styling – all in an efficient, contemporary size."
- 1983 Chrysler E Class

New Model: 1983 Chrysler Executive Sedan

1983 Chrysler Cordoba interior

New Model: 1983 Chrysler E Class

E Class & New Yorker have a 3" longer wheelbase than LeBaron

New Model: 1983 Chrysler New Yorker

Last Model Run: 1983 Chrysler Cordoba with Cabriolet Roof Package

1983 Chrysler Cordoba instrument panel

From the Brochure: "We've re-engineered the American luxury car. Compromise will never be part of the lifestyle of the people who are going places. They know that when they step out of a Chrysler Cordoba, they step out in style. They tell the world that individuality and common sense still exist."
- 1983 Chrysler Cordoba

1983 Chrysler LeBaron convertible with Mark Cross Package

1983 Chrysler LeBaron 4-door Sedan

From the Brochure: "Like no other cars in America, Europe or Japan. The Chrysler LeBarons have restored a feeling about an American car that's been missing for some time. The feeling: pride. The Chrysler Corporation is proud to build the LeBarons as the latest example of advanced automotive technology. We've focused a lot of our engineering expertise on making the LeBarons handsome, efficient front-wheel drive cars that are technically sound and luxurious." – 1983 Chrysler LeBaron

1983 Chrysler Town & Country

LeBaron instrumentation changes after 1982

1983 Chrysler LeBaron 2-door Coupe

Those 80s Cars – AMC & Chrysler

1983 - DODGE

1983 Dodge 400 Convertible

1983 Dodge 400 2-door

1983 Dodge 400 4-door

From the Brochure: "Owning one is like owning the road. Since its wheels first touched pavement last year, it has been obvious that Dodge 400 is an automobile with a singular purpose… to rekindle the pure enjoyment of driving.

Today Dodge 400 lineup offers a choice of three sporty front-wheel drive models, all designed with a canny awareness of energy economy.

For 1983, Dodge 400 offers, a four-passenger convertible and distinctive two- and four-door models."

- 1983 Dodge 400

New Model: 1983 Dodge 600 ES Sedan

Front-wheel drive, 2.2 liter 4-cylinder, 3-speed automatic, 103" wheelbase, 17 cu. ft. trunk, 24 estimated MPG, 32 MPG estimated highway

New Model: 1983 Dodge 600 Sedan

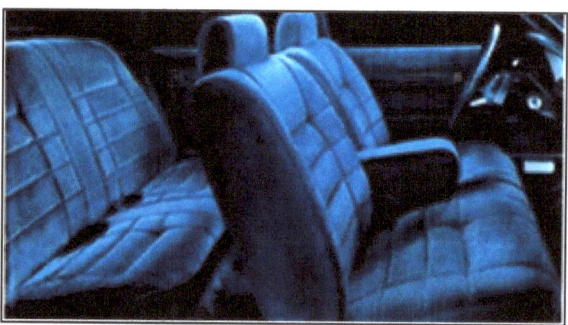
1983 Dodge 600 standard interior

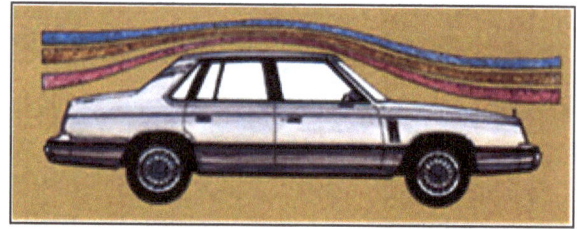

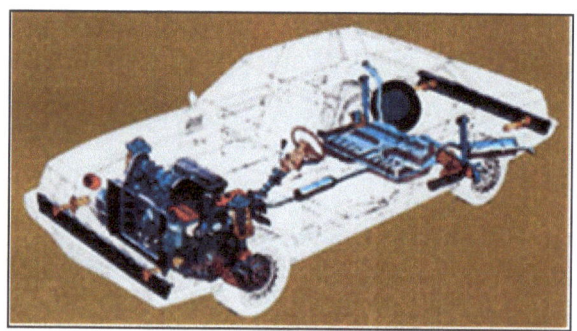

New 1.6 liter 4-cylinder engine introduced mid-year
1983 Dodge Charger

1983 Dodge Aries SE 2-door
2.2 liter 4-cylinder now standard

1983 Dodge Charger 2.2
New front storage and shift console. Sport suspension, 5-speed manual, & 14" Rallye wheels are standard

1983 Dodge Aries Wagon with Aries Sedan

1983 Dodge Charger instrument panel

New heater for improved distribution
1983 Dodge Aries SE interior

New Model: 1983 Dodge Shelby Charger

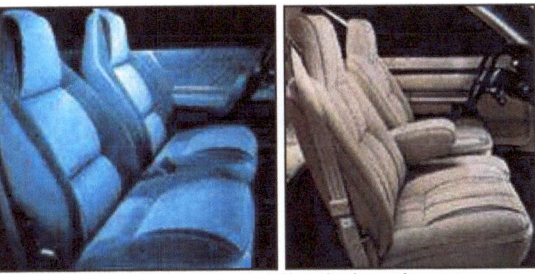
1983 Dodge Charger & Mirada interiors

Last Year Model: 1983 Dodge Mirada CMX

Those 80s Cars – AMC & Chrysler

1983 Dodge Diplomat Salon

1983 Dodge Omni

New 1.6 liter 4-cylinder engine introduced mid-year

1.4 liter 4-cylinder engine & 4-speed manual are standard

1983 Dodge Colt Custom

1983 Dodge Omni Custom

Colt offers 4 trim levels: base, Deluxe, Custom and RS

1983 Dodge Colt Custom RS

1983 Dodge Omni Custom interior

1983 Dodge Challenger Technica

1983 Dodge Rampage 2.2

From the Brochure: "At Dodge, driving excellence is engineered in. Design has a lot to do with the sophisticated formula that makes front-wheel drive technology work so well in the 1983 Dodge car lines. Not just make-it-look-nice styling, but aerodynamic styling that uses the flow of the air to hold the car to the road while maximizing engine power and fuel efficiency."

- 1983 Dodge

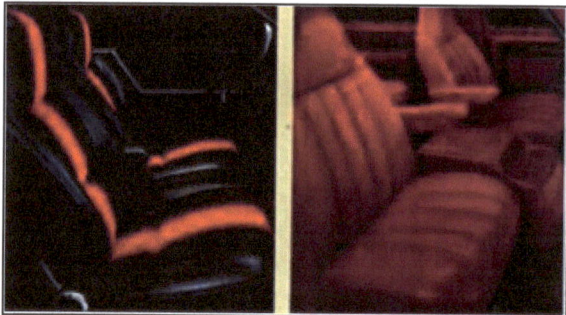
Rampage standard & deluxe interiors

Those 80s Cars – AMC & Chrysler

1983 - PLYMOUTH

1983 Plymouth Gran Fury

1983 Plymouth Gran Fury instrument panel

New 1.6 liter 4-cylinder engine introduced mid-year; 2.2 liter 4-cylinder optional

1983 Plymouth Turismo 2.2 & Scamp GT (back)

From the Brochure: "Zip on by the pump. The dashing good looks of a sporty car... the carry-all utility of a small truck... excellent performance... and equally excellent fuel economy. Put them all together and you get the all-new 1983 Plymouth Scamp."

- **New Model:** 1983 Plymouth Scamp

1983 Plymouth Scamp interior

1983 Plymouth Gran Fury interior

1983 Plymouth Turismo 2.2 interior

1983 Plymouth Turismo 2.2 interior

From the Brochure: "Turismo steps out with front-wheel drive efficiency that's packaged in sleek, distinctive sporty styling. The smart, spacious interior has room for five and standard front cloth-and-vinyl sport type high bucket seats for comfort and support."

- 1983 Plymouth Turismo

1983 Plymouth Reliant Special Edition 4-door Sedan

1983 Plymouth Reliant Special Edition interior

1983 Plymouth Reliant Special Edition Wagon

1983 Plymouth Special Edition 2-door Coupe

1983 Plymouth Horizon

New 1.6 liter 4-cylinder engine introduced mid-year

Last year's Champ is renamed Colt in 1983

1983 Plymouth Colt Custom RS 3-Door

1983 Plymouth Horizon Custom instrument panel

1983 Plymouth Sapporo Technica

New Technica Package with digital gauges

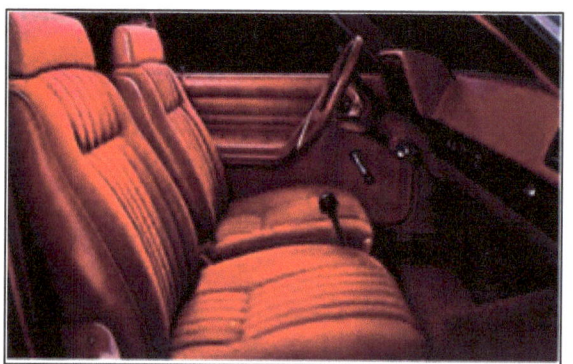
1983 Plymouth Horizon standard interior

1983 Plymouth Sapporo Technica dash panel

Those 80s Cars – AMC & Chrysler

1984

1984 - Facts at Glance

News Headlines

- Indria Ghandi is assassinated
- Summer Olympics held in LA
- French identify AIDS virus
- AT&T is broken up
- Apple Macintosh goes on sale
- CD players are introduced
- Michael Jackson's Thriller sells over 37 million copies

Tops in Pop Culture

Music
- When Doves Cry, Prince

Movies
- Ghost Busters

TV Show
- Dynasty

Sports Champions

Basketball
- Boston Celtics

Football
- L.A. Raiders

Baseball
- Detroit Tigers

Motor Trend – Car of the Year

Chevrolet Corvette

1984 - AMC / EAGLE

American Eagle Wagon

Luxury. Security. Unbeatable 4-Wheel Drive.

American Eagle is an automobile with the comfort and luxury of a fine road car, plus the capability to let you "shift-on-the-fly" to the confidence of 4-wheel drive. It's a well-appointed and equipped vehicle that's ready to take you and your family almost anywhere—in style and comfort—no matter what the road conditions.

Eagle has a powerful 4.2 liter, 6-cylinder engine with 5-speed manual transmission standard. But it's Eagle's luxurious interior that makes this elegant vehicle a pleasure to drive. There are individually reclining front seats in a choice of Deluxe grain vinyl or Highland Check fabric and conveniently positioned instruments and controls set in a color-keyed, woodgrain-accented instrument panel. In addition, there's a large selection of optional equipment and trim levels available in Eagle, offering the **feel** of a luxurious touring car.

With Eagle Limited, luxury is standard. There are reclining seats in supple leather, dual remote control mirrors, plush carpeting, wire wheel covers, and more.

So whichever Eagle model you select, 4-door Sedan, 4-door Eagle Wagon Sport or Wagon Limited, you'll find you have a vehicle that's roomy, comfortable, dependable and secure.

Enter the world of luxury 4-wheel drive with American Eagle.

1984 - CHRYSLER

1984 Chrysler Fifth Avenue

"New Yorker" name is dropped from the Fifth Avenue model in 1984 & the 5.2 liter (318 CID) V8 becomes standard

1984 Chrysler Fifth Avenue instrument panel

1984 Chrysler Fifth Avenue optional leather

New Model: 1984 Chrysler Laser XE Turbo

2.2 liter 4-cylinder is standard with a new optional turbocharger available

1984 Chrysler Laser interior

1984 Chrysler Laser XE instrument panel

2.2 liter 4-cylinder rated at 99 hp
2.2 turbo rated at 142 hp

1984 Chrysler LeBaron electronic instruments

New on convertible: rear side windows and top

1984 Chrysler LeBaron Town & Country Wagon & Convertible with woodgrain paneling
1984 Chrysler LeBaron Coupe, Sedan and Convertible

1984 Chrysler LeBaron Mark Cross interior

1984 Chrysler Executive Sedan

Limousine/Executive Sedan rear seat

Executive Sedan and Limousine have 40.2" of rear legroom

Limousine is 210.4" long with a 131" wheelbase

Executive Sedan is 203.4" long with a 124" wheelbase

Last Model Run: 1984 Chrysler E Class

E Class replaced in 1985 with Plymouth Caravelle

1984 Chrysler E Class split bench interior

1984 Chrysler New Yorker instrument panel

New digital instrumentation is standard on New Yorker in 1984

Refreshed: 1984 Chrysler New Yorker

1984 - DODGE

1984 Dodge 600 (last year's 400 Coupe & Convertible are re-badged as 600 this year)

Dodge Caravan, Daytona & 600 Convertible

New Model: 1984 Dodge Caravan

1984 Dodge Charger advertisement

New Model: 1984 Dodge Colt Vista Wagon

1.6 liter turbo 4-cylinder EFI, 102 hp

1984 Dodge Turbo Colt

1984 Dodge Diplomat SE interior

New Model: 1984 Dodge Conquest

1984 Dodge Conquest instrument panel

1984 Dodge Diplomat SE

1984 Dodge Aries SE 4-door Sedan

New Model: 1984 Dodge Daytona

New Trim Series: 1984 Dodge Omni GLH

1984 - PLYMOUTH

1984 Plymouth Gran Fury 4-door Sedan

1984 Plymouth Gran Fury interiors (standard bench above & optional 60/40 split bench)

New color-keyed bumper strips & side moldings
1984 Plymouth Reliant SE 4-door Sedan

1984 Plymouth full product line
New Models: Voyager & Colt Vista Wagon

1984 Plymouth Turismo

1984 Plymouth Horizon

1984 Plymouth Reliant SE Wagon

1985

1985 - Facts at Glance

News Headlines

- Live Aid concert raises $50 million for famine relief in Ethiopia
- 8.1 earthquake hits Mexico City
- Boris Becker becomes the youngest player to win Wimbledon, at 17 years old

Tops in Pop Culture

Music
- Careless Whisper, Wham! Featuring George Michael

Movies
- Back to the Future

TV Show
- The Cosby Show

Sports Champions

Basketball
- L.A. Lakers

Football
- San Francisco 49ers

Baseball
- Kansas City Royals

Motor Trend – Car of the Year

Volkswagen GTI

1985 - AMC / EAGLE

4.2 liter 6-cylinder engine with 5-speed manual transmission is standard equipment

1985 AMC Eagle Wagon

1985 - CHRYSLER

1985 Chrysler Fifth Avenue

Over 50 standard features on the Fifth Avenue

1985 Chrysler Fifth Avenue instrument panel

1985 Chrysler LeBaron Coupe, Convertible Sedan and Town & Country Wagon

LeBaron sports a revised grille. The 2.2 turbo engine gains 4 hp over last year's model.

1985 Chrysler LeBaron standard interior

1985 Chrysler New Yorker

1985 Chrysler New Yorker instrument panel

New push-button climate control introduced this year

1985 Chrysler New Yorker leather interior

1985 Chrysler LeBaron instrument Panel

Those 80s Cars – AMC & Chrysler

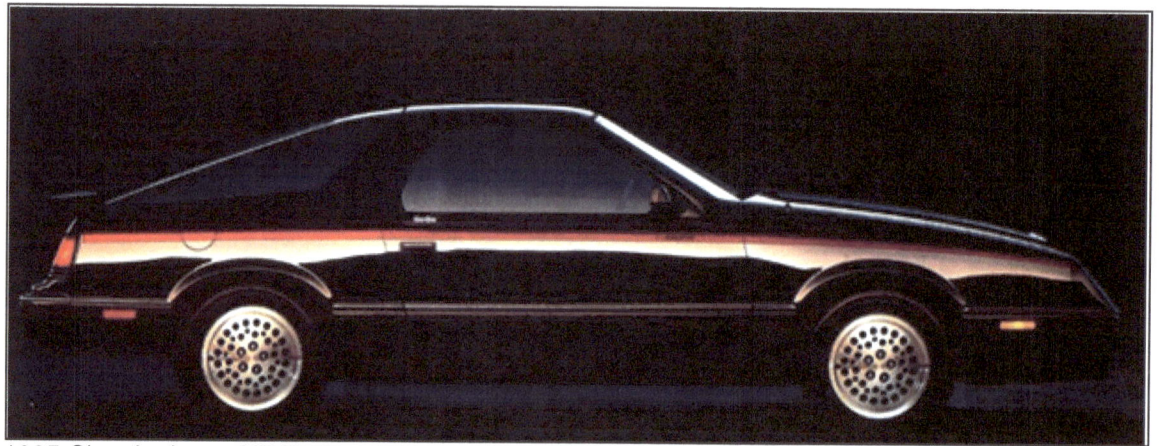
1985 Chrysler Laser XE Turbo

1985 Chrysler Laser optional leather interior

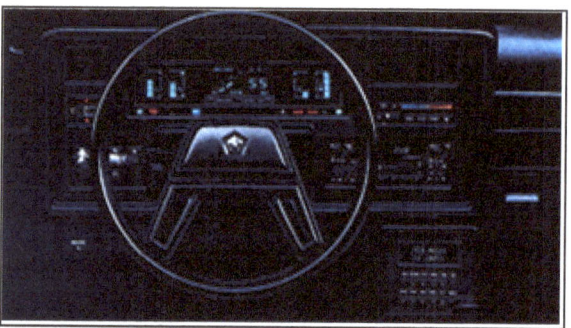
1985 Chrysler Laser instrument panel

.35 coefficient of drag

New Model: 1985 Chrysler LeBaron GTS

1985 Chrysler Limousine

Those 80s Cars – AMC & Chrysler

1985 - DODGE

New Model: 1985 Dodge Lancer ES

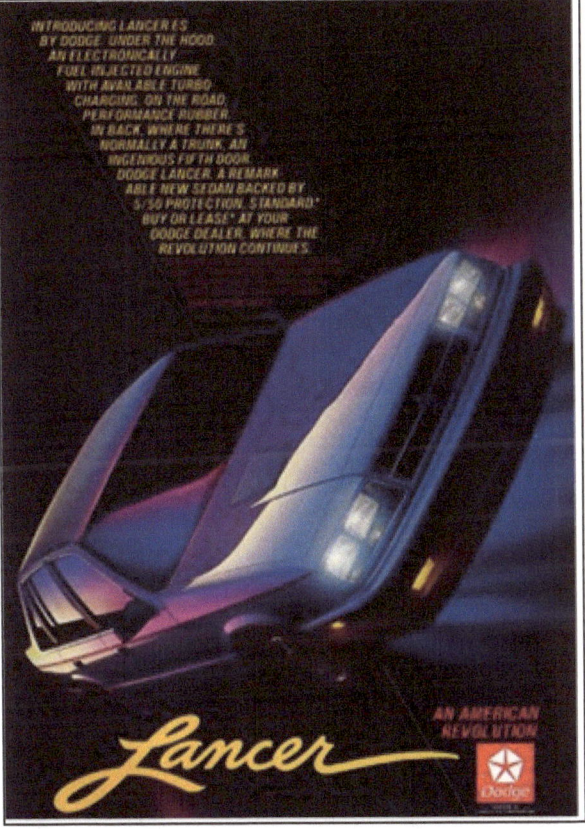

2.2 liter OHC multi-point EFI 4-cylinder 99hp
2.2 liter OHC multi-point EFI 4-cylinder turbo 146hp
with 5-speed manual or 3-speed auto

1985 Dodge 600 4-door Sedan

1985 Dodge 600 Club Coupe

1985 Dodge Aries SE Wagon

1985 Dodge Diplomat SE 4-door Sedan

3 trim series: Omni, Omni SE, Omni GLH

1985 Dodge Omni

3 trim series: Daytona, Daytona Turbo & Daytona Turbo Z
Turbo Z: 0-50 in 5.51 seconds

1985 Dodge Daytona Turbo Z

145hp 2.6 liter turbo 4

1985 Dodge Conquest

1985 Dodge Colt E 5-Door & 3-Door Hatchbacks

2.0 liter 4-cylinder

1985 Dodge Colt Vista Wagon

1985 Dodge Colt Premier 4-door Sedan

Those 80s Cars – AMC & Chrysler

1985 - PLYMOUTH

1985 Plymouth model line

1985 Plymouth Voyager LE

1985 Plymouth Horizon

1985 Plymouth Turismo Duster

1985 Plymouth Reliant LE Coupe & Sedan

1985 Plymouth Reliant Coupe, Sedan, Wagon

1985 Plymouth Gran Fury Salon

1985 Plymouth Colt

1985 Plymouth Conquest

1985 Plymouth Caravelle replaces 1984's Chrysler E Class

New Model: 1985 Plymouth Caravelle SE

Those 80s Cars – AMC & Chrysler

1986

1986 - Facts at Glance

News Headlines

- SALT signed
- Chernobyl nuclear accident
- Iran-Contra Affair begins
- Mike Tyson becomes youngest heavyweight champion
- UK & France announce plans for Channel Tunnel
- Shuttle Challenger disaster

Tops in Pop Culture

Music
- That's What Friends Are For, Dionne & Friends

Movies
- Top Gun

TV Show
- The Cosby Show

Sports Champions

Basketball
- Boston Celtics

Football
- Chicago Bears

Baseball
- N.Y. Mets

Motor Trend – Car of the Year

Ford Taurus LX

1986 - AMC / EAGLE

1986 - CHRYSLER

1986 Chrysler LeBaron GTS

1986 Chrysler Laser

New 2.5 liter EFI engine

New roof treatment

Refreshed: 1986 Chrysler New Yorker

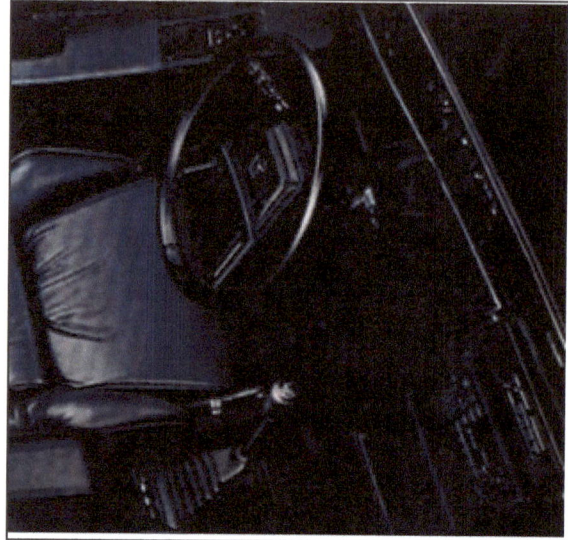
1986 Chrysler Laser optional leather interior

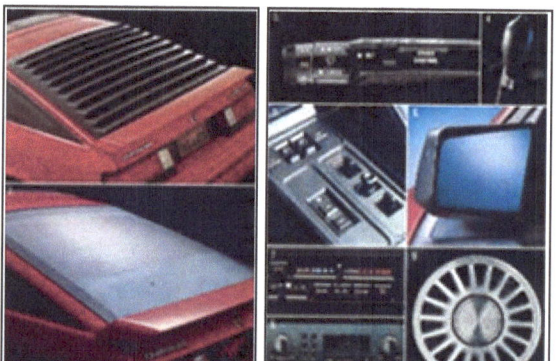
1986 Chrysler Laser accessories

1986 Chrysler New Yorker leather interior

1986 Chrysler New Yorker instrument panel

66   Those 80s Cars – AMC & Chrysler

Refreshed: 1986 Chrysler Town & Country

1986 Town & Country Mark Cross leather interior

Refreshed & Last Model Run: 1986 Chrysler LeBaron Sedan

1986 Chrysler LeBaron instrument panel

Refreshed & Last Model Run: 1986 Chrysler Convertible

New 2.5 liter EFI engine option

Refreshed & Last Model Run: 1986 Chrysler LeBaron Coupe

1986 Chrysler Fifth Avenue

1986 Chrysler LeBaron interior

Those 80s Cars – AMC & Chrysler

1986 - DODGE

1986 Dodge Lancer ES

1986 Dodge Lancer ES electronic instruments

1986 Dodge Lancer ES available leather interior

1986 Dodge Daytona Turbo Z

From the Brochure: "In the realm of front-drive technology, Dodge challenges any other car company in the world. And Dodge has the world's largest fleet of turbocharged cars. The strength of these two statements translates directly into the strength of the products we are building today. Our commitment to front-drive technology enables us to build cars that are lighter, more space-efficient and more fuel-efficient." - 1986 Dodge

1986 Dodge Daytona

1986 Dodge Daytona Turbo Z leather interior

1986 Dodge Daytona Turbo Z

1986 Dodge Conquest

From the Brochure: "The credentials that define a performance sports car are multidimensional. In addition to outright speed, it must have open-road agility. Handling must be precise. Aerodynamics must work with the car. There must be outstanding stability under all conditions of braking and deceleration. The interior must be driver-oriented. In short, it must be a car in total balance."
 - 1986 Dodge Daytona

Refreshed & Last Year Model: 1986 Dodge 600 convertible

1986 Dodge Aries K LE 4-door Sedan

Aries K models include 2-doors and 4-doors in 3 trim series: base Aries K, elegant Aries K SE and luxurious Aries K LE. Wagons available in SE and LE trim levels only.

Refreshed & Last Year Model: 1986 Dodge 600 2-door Coupe

1986 Dodge Diplomat SE

1986 Dodge 600 SE 4-door interior

1986 Dodge Diplomat SE interior

1986 Dodge Colt E Sedan & Hatchback

1986 Dodge Charger 2.2 (back) & Charger

1986 Dodge Colt Vista 4WD Wagon

1986 Dodge Omni SE

Those 80s Cars – AMC & Chrysler

1986 - PLYMOUTH

1986 Plymouth Reliant K LE 2-door Coupe

1986 Plymouth Reliant K LE 4-door Sedan

1986 Plymouth Reliant K SE Wagon

1986 Plymouth Reliant K instrument panel

1986 Plymouth Reliant K LE interior

1986 Plymouth Caravelle SE 4-door Sedan

New, optional 2.5 liter 4-cylinder with dual balance shafts

1986 Plymouth Caravelle SE 4-door Sedan

From the Brochure: "Style and value come together in today's most exciting family transportation, the 1986 Plymouth Caravelle SE. Caravelle SE is Plymouth's finest, combining six-passenger comfort with crisp handling and front-wheel drive."
– 1986 Plymouth Caravelle

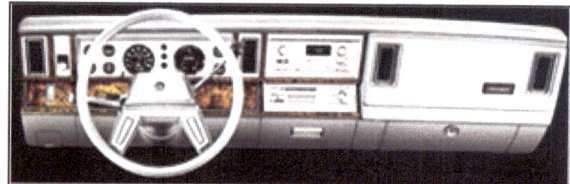
1986 Plymouth Caravelle SE instrument panel

1986 Plymouth Caravelle SE interior

1986 Plymouth Horizon

1986 Plymouth Turismo 2.2

1986 Plymouth Turismo 2.2 instrument panel (Rallye instrument cluster)

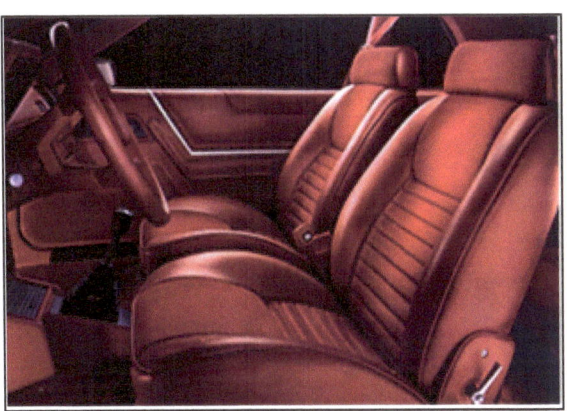
1986 Plymouth Turismo 2.2 interior

1986 Plymouth Gran Fury Salon (Standard 5.2 liter V8)

1986 Plymouth Gran Fury Salon interior with optional velour and vinyl 60/40 front bench seat

1986 Plymouth Conquest/Colt Vista 4WD Wagon

1986 Plymouth Colt Sedan

Those 80s Cars – AMC & Chrysler

1987

1987- Facts at Glance

News Headlines

- Oct 19 Stock Market crashes $508, dropping 22.6%
- Fox broadcasting debuts
- Televangelist Jim Bakker scandal breaks

Tops in Pop Culture

Music
- Walk Like an Egyptian, Bangles

Movies
- 3 Men and a Baby

TV Show
- The Cosby Show

Sports Champions

Basketball
- L.A. Lakers

Football
- N.Y. Giants

Baseball
- Minnesota Twins

Motor Trend – Car of the Year

Ford Thunderbird Turbo Coupe

1987 - AMC / EAGLE

1987 AMC / Eagle Wagon & Sedan

The performance and dependability of four-wheel drive. A sophisticated, soothing interior. The convenience of cargo space and superb trailering capabilities. Quite simply, Eagle's got it all.

Whether you choose Eagle wagon or sedan, you're making a very intelligent choice. Both come with an impressive list of standard features designed to give you maximum security and comfort. In addition, an extensive list of optional features lets you equip your Eagle to suit your needs.

Through the years, Eagle heritage has grown strong and proud. 1987 is no exception. Eagle truly is a breed apart.

1987 - CHRYSLER

1987 Chrysler Fifth Avenue

1987 Chrysler New Yorker

1987 Chrysler Fifth Avenue optional leather interior

1987 Chrysler New Yorker leather interior

1987 Chrysler New Yorker instrument panel

1987 Chrysler Fifth Avenue instrument panel

From the Brochure: "A respect for tradition. That's what keeps classical New Yorker luxuriously comfortable. A resolve to improve. That's what makes contemporary New Yorker powerfully efficient. A union of the established and the innovative; a collaboration of the familiar and refined. That's how New Yorker became the ultimate high-technology luxury sedan."
- 1987 Chrysler New Yorker

1987 Chrysler LeBaron 4-door Sedan

1987 Chrysler LeBaron, Town & Country Wagon

1987 Chrysler LeBaron GTS

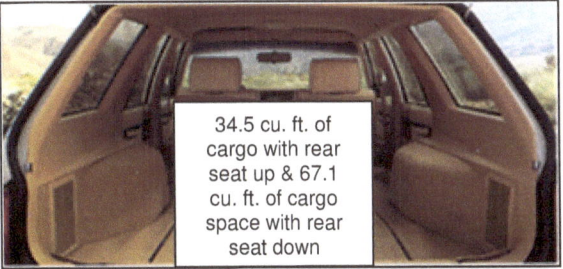
1987 Chrysler Town & Country Wagon

34.5 cu. ft. of cargo with rear seat up & 67.1 cu. ft. of cargo space with rear seat down

New Model: 1987 Chrysler Conquest (previously Plymouth & Dodge Conquest)

From the Brochure: "The 1987 Chrysler Town & Country Station Wagon continues to be a successful combination of traditional station wagon features, Chrysler's advanced front-wheel drive technology and Chrysler quality backed by the 5/50 Limited Warranty. Refinements for 1987 include a standard long-life stainless steel exhaust system, standard electronic instrument cluster and a new available electronic speed control for easier use during highway cruising."
- 1987 Chrysler Town & Country

1987 Chrysler Town & Country optional Mark Cross leather interior

Those 80s Cars – AMC & Chrysler

THE ALL-NEW CHRYSLER LE BARON.
BEAUTY... WITH A PASSION FOR DRIVING.

Shaped by wind, reason and a unique artistry, the design of the all-new LeBaron coupe is more than efficient aerodynamics...it is a triumph of elegance.

While the new LeBaron believes in cheating the wind, it has no intention of robbing the eye...It is an image of arresting beauty.

But beneath this beauty breathes a passion. LeBaron was created to drive. And drive it does! It attacks the road with a high torque, 2.5 fuel-injected engine. Its turbo option can blur the surface of any passing lane.

Handling is equally impressive. LeBaron's advanced front-wheel drive and positive-response suspension will calm the most demanding roads.

Even razor-sharp turns lose their menace.

Luxurious contoured leather seats comfort and support. Instrument readings are captured in a glance. Controls, positioned to minimize distraction.

And whether you buy or lease, LeBaron gives you Chrysler's new protection plan* that covers powertrain, engine and turbo for 7 years or 70,000 miles. And against outerbody rust-through for 7 years or 100,000 miles.

Its power will move you. Its beauty will stop you. The all-new Chrysler LeBaron. At your Chrysler-Plymouth dealer.

CHRYSLER. DRIVING TO BE THE BEST.

New Model: 1987 Chrysler LeBaron Coupe

From the Brochure: "LeBaron is a car for drivers who enjoy the roadway. It is a car to be appreciated by those who favor touches of luxury and convenience."

- 1987 Chrysler LeBaron Coupe

1987 - DODGE

1987 Dodge Diplomat SE

1987 Dodge 600 4-door Sedan

1987 Dodge Diplomat SE interior

1987 Dodge 600 SE 4-door interior

1987 Dodge Aries K LE 2-door Coupe

Lowest priced car of its class made in America
1987 Dodge Omni America

1987 Dodge Omni interior

1987 Dodge Shelby Charger (back) & Charger

Those 80s Cars – AMC & Chrysler

New Model: 1987 Dodge Shadow 2-door Coupe

45 standard features; more than any other car of its size

New Model: 1987 Dodge Shadow 4-door Sedan

1987 Dodge Shadow ES interior

1987 Dodge Caravan SE

1987 Dodge Caravan LE interior

1987 Dodge Lancer ES

3 trims series: Daytona, Daytona Pacifica, Daytona Shelby Z

Refreshed:
1987 Dodge Daytona Shelby Z

1987 Dodge Daytona Pacifica interior

1987 Dodge Colt Premier 4-door Sedan

1987 Dodge Colt E 3-Door Hatchback

1987 Dodge Colt Vista 4WD Wagon

1987 - PLYMOUTH

2.2 liter 4-cylinder standard
2.5 liter 4-cylinder optional

New Model: 1987 Plymouth Sundance 4-door (also available in coupe)

1987 Plymouth Caravelle SE 4-door

1987 Plymouth Reliant K LE 4-door Sedan

1987 Sundance Options

1987 Plymouth Reliant K LE interior

1987 Plymouth Gran Fury Salon

1987 Plymouth Gran Fury Salon

1987 Plymouth Colt Sedan

1987 Plymouth Colt Turbo instrument panel

1987 Plymouth Colt Vista 4WD Wagon

1987 Plymouth Conquest

1987 Plymouth Colt Hatchback

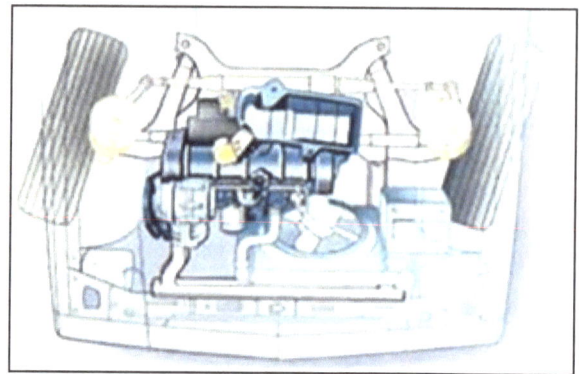

1987 Plymouth Turismo

1987 Plymouth Turismo

1987 Plymouth Horizon America

1988

1988 Facts at Glance

News Headlines

- Iran/Iraq war ends
- Terrorist blow up Pan Am jet over Lockerbie
- Hubble space telescope placed in orbit
- Stealth bomber unveiled

Tops in Pop Culture

Music
- Faith, George Michael

Movies
- Rain Man

TV Show
- The Cosby Show

Sports Champions

Basketball
- L.A. Lakers

Football
- Washington Redskins

Baseball
- L.A. Dodgers

Motor Trend – Car of the Year

Pontiac Grand Prix

1988 - AMC / EAGLE

New Model: 1988 Eagle Premier ES – Now owned by Chrysler, Chrysler re-brands the franchise as Eagle and sells models from Renault, the previous owner of AMC/Eagle.

2.5 liter 4-cylinder engine with 4-speed automatic overdrive transmission is standard equipment

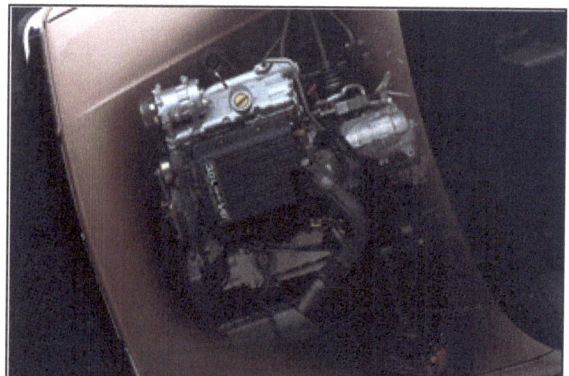

1988 Eagle Premier optional all-aluminum 3.0 liter V6 engine with multi-port fuel injection

Eagle Premier LX interior

Last Model Run: 1988 Eagle Wagon, formerly AMC Eagle

New Model: 1988 Eagle Premier ES

1988 - CHRYSLER

The New "New Yorkers" comes with a 3.0 V6

(from left)
New Models: 1988 Chrysler New Yorker Landau & New Yorker
Last Model Run: 1998 New Yorker Turbo (for 1988, this body style comes with the 2.2 turbo only)
1988 Chrysler Fifth Avenue

> **From the Brochure:** "Luxury abounds. Prestigious, comfortably quiet, smoothly maneuverable luxury… in Chrysler's all-new New Yorker Landau. Distinctively styled in the traditional big-car manner. Accented with such elegant touches as a classically graceful grille and concealed headlights. Engineered for stability with front-wheel drive; for performance with V-6 power; for comfort and quiet with road-smoothing suspension. And for the most discriminating and demanding drivers, a most extensive list of standard features."
>
> - 1988 Chrysler New Yorker Landau

1988 Chrysler New Yorker Landau interior

1988 Chrysler New Yorker Turbo leather interior

1988 Chrysler New Yorker standard interior

> **From the Brochure:** "The New Yorker's suspension is tuned to provide a smooth, comfortable ride. In addition, a variable front-strut damping system helps reduce the noise and jarring effects of road hazards. Comfort prevails."   – 1988 Chrysler New Yorker

1988 Chrysler Fifth Avenue leather interior

1988 Chrysler LeBaron Convertible, LeBaron Coupe, and LeBaron GTS
Last Model Run: 1988 LeBaron Sedan and LeBaron Town & Country Wagon

1988 Chrysler LeBaron Premium Convertible

Its power will move you.
Its beauty will stop you.

1988 Chrysler GTS Premium optional leather interior

1988 Chrysler LeBaron Premium interior with optional leather seating

1988 Chrysler LeBaron 4-door sedan interior with available bucket seats

1988 Chrysler Conquest

1988 Chrysler LeBaron Town & Country optional Mark Cross leather interior

Those 80s Cars – AMC & Chrysler

1988 - DODGE

2.5 liter 4-cylinder standard with available 3.0 liter multipoint fuel-injected V6

New Model: 1988 Dodge Dynasty LE Sedan

1988 Dodge Dynasty LE interior

1988 Dodge Dynasty features & options

1988 Dodge Shadow ES 2-door

1988 Dodge Shadow ES 4-door

1988 Dodge Shadow ES interior

1988 Dodge Daytona Shelby Z

1988 Dodge Lancer ES

New 7/70 Power Train & 7/100 Anti-Corrosion Warranties

1988 Dodge Aries America LE 4-door

1988 Dodge Aries America LE 2-door

1988 Dodge 600 & 600 SE (back)

Fuel injection now standard

1988 Dodge Diplomat SE

1988 Dodge Omni America

1988 Dodge Colt Premier Turbo Sedan

1988 Dodge Colt DL 2-door Hatchback

1988 Dodge Colt Vista 4WD Wagon

1988 - PLYMOUTH

Last Model Run: 1988 Plymouth Caravelle SE

1988 Plymouth Reliant America LE 4-Door

1988 Plymouth Caravelle SE interior

1988 Plymouth Reliant America LE 2-Door

1988 Plymouth Sundance RS

1988 Plymouth Reliant interior

1988 Plymouth Sundance

1988 Plymouth Sundance Turbo RS

Plymouth

Colt Vista

1988 Plymouth Horizon America interior

Fuel injection now standard

1988 Plymouth Colt Premier Turbo 4-Door

1988 Plymouth Horizon America

1988 Plymouth Colt E 3-Door　　　Colt DL 4-Door　　　Colt Turbo 3-Door

1988 Plymouth Colt DL 3-Door

1989

1989 - Facts at Glance

News Headlines

- USSR pulls out of Afghanistan
- George Bush Sr inaugurated as President
- Exxon Valdez spills 240,000 barrels of oil
- Leona Helmsley convicted on tax fraud
- Ford buys Jaguar
- Berlin Wall comes down

Tops in Pop Culture

Music
- Look Away, Chicago

Movies
- Batman

TV Show
- Roseanne

Sports Champions

Basketball
- Detroit Pistons

Football
- San Francisco 49ers

Baseball
- Oakland A's

Motor Trend – Car of the Year

Ford Thunderbird SC

1989 - AMC / EAGLE

1989 Eagle Premier ES Limited

1989 Eagle Summit optional 1.6 liter 16-valve DOHC

New Model: 1989 Eagle Summit LX Sedan

1989 Eagle Summit LX interior

2.2 liter 4-cylinder electronically fuel-injected, independent rear suspension, front-wheel drive

1989 Eagle Medallion LX Sedan (previously sold as Renault Medallion in '87 & '88)

Optional 3rd row forward-facing seat

1989 Eagle Medallion DL Wagon

1989 Eagle Medallion DL interior

1989 - CHRYSLER

New Model: 1989 Chrysler's TC by Maserati

From the Brochure: "Style is beauty… and performance. The best of two traditions. A blend of Italian craftsmanship and American engineering. The result is the TC… Chrysler's Turbo Convertible built by Maserati. TC is a luxury sport coupe whose stunning style is hand-hewn by Maserati coachworkers who meticulously form, fit and finish automobiles… as if each were one of a kind. The style of its appearance is enhanced on the road by Chrysler engineering… whose refinements include a gas-charged touring suspension system." – 1989 Chrysler's TC by Maserati

1989 Chrysler LeBaron GTS Turbo

1989 Chrysler LeBaron GTS optional leather interior

1989 Chrysler LeBaron Convertible

1989 Chrysler LeBaron Coupe

1989 Chrysler New Yorker Landau

1989 New Yorker introduces Chrysler's new 4-speed, fully adaptive electronic control Ultradrive transaxle

1989 Chrysler New Yorker Landau optional leather interior

Last Model Run: 1989 Chrysler Fifth Avenue

1989 Chrysler New Yorker

1989 Chrysler New Yorker interior

Last Model Run: 1989 Chrysler Fifth Avenue

1989 Chrysler Fifth Avenue optional leather interior

Those 80s Cars – AMC & Chrysler

1989 - DODGE

1989 Dodge Dynasty LE

From the Brochure: "Dynasty and Dynasty LE. An artful blend of time-honored heritage and state-of-the-art technology. Bringing together such traditional family sedan qualities as impressive ride."
- 1989 Dodge Dynasty

1989 Dodge Caravan LE & Caravan SE

New Model: 1989 Dodge Spirit ES

New Model: 1989 Dodge Spirit ES

1989 Dodge Caravan LE optional leather interior

From the Brochure: "Available with an array of performance engines, such as the 2.5-liter turbo. With multipoint fuel-injection. Four cylinders. Single overhead cam. And a turbocharger that responds quickly to provide low- and mid-range performance, such as 150 horsepower at 4,800 RPM."
- 1989 Dodge Spirit

Power Trip
1989 Dodge Lancer Shelby

Exclusive Appeal
Last Model Run: 1989 Dodge Diplomat SE

Generous Value
Last Model Run: 1989 Dodge Aries America

Great Value
1989 Dodge Omni America

1989 Dodge Colt DL 4WD Wagon

Wild
1989 Dodge Daytona

1989 Dodge Shadow Coupe

1989 Dodge Shadow interior

Affordable quality from Japan. Dodge Colt.
1989 Dodge Colt E

1989 Dodge Colt Vista 4WD Wagon

1989 - PLYMOUTH

Available 3.0 liter V6 with Ultradrive fully adaptive 4-speed automatic

New Model: 1989 Plymouth Acclaim LX

1989 Plymouth Acclaim LX interior

From the Brochure: "Abundant room and comfort in a midsize car, front-wheel drive, and more than 50 standard features help make the Acclaim the optimum family vehicle." – 1989 Plymouth Acclaim

1989 Plymouth Sundance RS Sedan

New 2.5 liter Turbo I MPI engine option

1989 Plymouth Sundance RS Coupe

1989 Plymouth Sundance RS interior

Those 80s Cars – AMC & Chrysler

1989 Plymouth Horizon America & **Last Model Run:** 1989 Plymouth Reliant America (back)

1989 Plymouth Reliant America interior

1.6 liter 16-valve DOHC turbo MPI 4-cylinder engine

1989 Plymouth Colt GT Turbo

1989 Plymouth Colt DL 4WD Wagon

1989 Plymouth Omni America interior

1989 Plymouth Colt Vista 4WD Wagon

96   Those 80s Cars – AMC & Chrysler

Index

Table of Contents 2
Foreword 3
The 80's Measured 4

1980 5
   1980 - Facts at Glance 5
   1980 - AMC / EAGLE 6
   1980 - CHRYSLER 8
   1980 - DODGE 11
   1980 - PLYMOUTH 13

1981 15
   1981 - Facts at Glance 15
   1981 - AMC / EAGLE 16
   1981 - CHRYSLER / IMPERIAL 18
   1981 - DODGE 21
   1981 - PLYMOUTH 25

1982 27
   1982 - Facts at Glance 27
   1982 - AMC / EAGLE 28
   1982 - CHRYSLER / IMPERIAL 30
   1982 - DODGE 32
   1982 - PLYMOUTH 34

1983 36
   1983 - Facts at Glance 36
   1983 - AMC / EAGLE 37
   1983 - CHRYSLER / IMPERIAL 39
   1983 - DODGE 42
   1983 - PLYMOUTH 45

1984 47
   1984 - Facts at Glance 47
   1984 - AMC / EAGLE 48
   1984 - CHRYSLER 49
   1984 - DODGE 51
   1984 - PLYMOUTH 54

1985 55
   1985 - Facts at Glance 55
   1985 - AMC / EAGLE 56
   1985 - CHRYSLER 57
   1985 - DODGE 59
   1985 - PLYMOUTH 62

1986 64
   1986 - Facts at Glance 64
   1986 - AMC / EAGLE 65
   1986 - CHRYSLER 66
   1986 - DODGE 68
   1986 - PLYMOUTH 70

1987 72
   1987- Facts at Glance 72
   1987 - AMC / EAGLE 73
   1987 - CHRYSLER 74
   1987 - DODGE 77
   1987 - PLYMOUTH 79

1988...81
    1988 Facts at Glance..81
    1988 - AMC / EAGLE 82
    1988 - CHRYSLER 83
    1988 - DODGE..85
    1988 - PLYMOUTH 87

1989...89
    1989 - Facts at Glance 89
    1989 - AMC / EAGLE 90
    1989 - CHRYSLER 91
    1989 - DODGE..93
    1989 - PLYMOUTH 95

Index 97

www.ingramcontent.com/pod-product-compliance
Lightning Source LLC
Chambersburg PA
CBHW040912020526

44116CB00026B/33